Feelings from Within

Shamarel Allen

PAGE PUBLISHING
Conneaut Lake, PA

First originally published by Page Publishing 2023

ISBN 978-1-6624-2850-0 (pbk)
ISBN 978-1-6624-2851-7 (digital)

Printed in the United States of America

Goes out to Tonia R. Warren (Tonia Boo). Tonia Boo was my cousin, but we grew up like sisters. She gave me good support and spoke strong, encouraging words. At the age of twenty-two, the Lord called for her to come home to be with him. Tonia Boo is gone in flesh, but her spirit lives on inside of me.

Believe in yourself.

Building One Up

Building one up
Starts with a made-up mind
Letting the fears go and making
The courage grow
One will have a clear mind
Willing to seek a new change at life
Building one up
Will be guided with their spirits
And lead from the Lord
As one's eyes begin to open
New things they will see
Things that they were missing out on before
If one just wanted to move forward
To get a new start at life
Learning and doing new things
Succeeding will come to store
To start on this journey land
One must have a made-up mind
Believing in yourself and
Faith in the Lord
Building one up

God will help me.

In His Hands

The power of prayer
Is strong indeed
For the Lord above
Can hear our needs
When times get hard
One gets depressed
Just let go and
Fall to your knees
For the Lord can hear
All that one say
Speak from within
And believe in faith
Not a moment too soon
Or too late
The things that we prayed
Have fallen in place
In his hand

Never give up.

Living a Dream

We all have dream, goals and desires
That we want to reach
It's just the dos and don'ts
Not knowing what to do or
The right steps to take
That is holding one back
Living a dream can have one
Smiling in their sleep, making things
Seem like it's easy to reach
Sometimes one goes through a phase
A phase of doubt, letting the words "I can't"
Sit in their head
"I can't" is not a joyful word
Only doubtful
If one will let go, take heed
Go after their goals and desires
They want to reach
Then one can proceed
But if not, one will only
Continue to smile in their sleep
Living a dream, they wish
To reach

I will not give up.

Focus

Focus on your desire
To reach your goals
Focus on pushing yourself forward
So that you can succeed
One may fall back
Their load maybe too heavy to carry
Or one is focusing on others' needs and their things as well
To get back on track
One must put a shield on
Each side of their face
Block the distraction from others
And keep one from looking back
Trying to see their load
One must then tell themselves
"I must focus on me"
Meaning, mind and eyes
Focus on me
So I can achieve my desires and mission
Of accomplishing my goals
Focus

Focus on your goals.

A Step Away

Aiming for goals can be a step away
Reaching out and helping others
Can also take place
As one sits back and thinks about their plans
What are the dos and don'ts for this journey land?
While striving to proceed, one takes a fall
But with God's help, He'll do it all
While holding on and not giving up
You may have reached the high point
One or two steps away
Now one can say,
"I'm getting closer and closer each day"
Aiming for goals
A step away

I will overcome all stumbling blocks.

A Spinning Wheel

Our life that we live
Is like a wheel
That spins in a circle
On the hour after hour
A wheel can only spin
How fast or slow we want it to go
When one is having problems
Building all up inside
Not aware that the wheel is
Spinning faster and faster
To slow that wheel down
Is like releasing stress
Give it to God
Let him do the rest
If a wheel stops or loses a turn
It's another way of saying
We fall but we must not quit
So spin that wheel again and
In the outcome, with God's help
You'll win on
A spinning wheel

Blessings will come.

God Did It

As I went to church, listening to a pastor preach
I felt like he was talking to me
Opening of my eyes allowed me to see
God did it
When one was worried, stressed out
Wondering how they will pay their bills
After a letter came in the mail
Opened it up, a check was there
God did it
One wants to buy a house, but their credit wasn't good enough
After going to pay the rent, the paperwork was there
God did it
Some people will misjudge other kids
Say that they will never become anything
But when one went back to school
Receiving their bachelor's degree
God did it
If someone asks you
"How did you make it?" Or
"What did you do to get through?"
Just turn and look at them and say
God did it

I am full of excitement.

Doing It BIG

Another year is here, I will be making a change
Putting my pain and hurt behind me
That was done from others
A new start I will begin
I will be doing it b.i.g
Doing it b.i.g to have stronger faith
Doing it b.i.g to have a new car in the yard
Doing it b.i.g to buy a house
Doing it b.i.g to have strong determination
Doing it b.i.g to put money aside for hard times
I will be doing it b.i.g
Others can also do it b.i.g
By telling themselves "I can"
And use the meaning of b.i.g
<u>B</u>elieve <u>i</u>n <u>G</u>od
Doing it by believing in him

Make a joyful noise.

Casting a Line

As one goes out fishing in their boat
Patiently waiting for a
Fish to bite their hook
Looking for a good companion
One was still waiting on a fish
He then felt a snag
So he rolls the line in
Nothing was there
So he cast the line out
Farther the line went
Patiently waiting for
Another fish bites
Strong real companion
He felt a strong snag roll the line in
Thinking that the snag was a bass, but
It was me instead
His good strong, real companion
As one gets older
And may stop fishing
As long as there's water in the sea
I'll always have love for you
And hook on thee

Sunshine is all around me.

Brighter on the Other Side

It comes a time in life when we
All go through trials and tribulations
Not knowing what to do or the
Right steps to take
Causing one to feel like they
Want to give up, letting the words
"Is he there?" sit in
Their heads or have one wonder
If they are all alone
If one will just hold on
And believe in him
God will be there to help you get through
On the other side, he will carry you to
Where there are much brighter lights,
Joyfulness within and happiness
That will never end
Brighter on the other side
Starts with God and faith
So let it begin
Brighter on the other side

I will have a smile on my face.

Colors from Above

Colors from above shine bright
In the blue skies
On a clear, sunny day
Birds flying in the sky
Bees buzzing around flowers
Whistle in the wind occur
Colors from above
Leaves falling from the trees
Blowing left and right
Kids running outside to play
On this warm beautiful day
Colors from above
Fishermen throw rods out
From their boat
Others walking, laughing, just having fun
Looking up above to see the colors
A rainbow in the sky

Joy is all around me.

That Time of Year

That time of year
Is when the spring is here
The grass gets greener and the flowers begin to grow
As we watch our kids
go out and play
On a warm beautiful day
Playing ball, running around
Laughing and making loud sounds
That time of year
Is when one begins to plant
Their colorful flowers in their bed
Sitting outside in their rocking chairs
Watching the birds fly around, bees making a
Buzzing sound and listening to the whistle from the wind
That time of year is now

Humble yourself.

A Whistle in the Night

As one was walking in the middle of the night
A whistle sound one heard
Stars sparkling in the night, the moon round and white
A whistle in the night
Birds was chirping, trees were blowing left to right
Leaves falling to the ground
One then begins to hear animal sounds
A whistle in the night
When one reaches their final stop to lay their head down
Slowly closing their eyes to rest
While listening to
A whistle in the night

Believe in the goodness of the Lord.

A Sparkle in the Sky

While out in the night
Walking along the beach
Listening to the whistle
Of the wind and
Birds chirping softly
It was a sparkle
In the sky
As I looked up
High above the trees
The stars were shining bright
Deep down inside, I
Felt good and relieved
Knowing that it was him
Our Heavenly Father
Watching over me
I wasn't alone or afraid
For he can, too, be at your side
If one grabs and takes heed
Just stand back and look up
One then can see
A sparkle in the sky

The Lord is my strength.

Angels in the Sky

That time has come
When they meet up again
Reaching their final stop
Their home that is
"Heaven in the sky"
Now that they are free
From sickness and stress
They will spread their wings out
And guide the rest
Give us a positive attitude
And a made-up mind, making
Us feel good at the same time
But if one shall start to feel
Discouraged, wanting to quit
Stop for a moment, look up
Say a few words to your
Angels in the sky

I can do all things through
the power of God.

Side by Side

They became one
When they stood
Side by side,
Facing each other, holding hands
Saying the two words "I do"
Side by side
Their relationship grew and grew
Until they became an older couple
If one was feeling down, become sick, had pain or just
Needed someone to talk to
He would be by her side
Or she at his
Side by side
Now that they are both gone
Resting in peace
Together they lay
Side by side

I will follow the steps of the Lord.

They're Free

When a loved one or close friend
Has passed away, it was God calling
For them to come home to be with him
They're free
Free from all the pain, hurt, and
weakness held within
Free from all the wear
and tear put on their body
They're free
Memories of them will be there
Family functions we all shared
when they were there
The visits and the phone calls among us
Now it's time for family and friends
To accept that they're gone
to their new home to be with the Lord
But their spirit will live on now that
They're free

Think positive.

Our Angel in the Sky

It comes a time in life
When our love must go
That time has now come, the Lord called for
One to come home and be with him
Our angel in the sky
It's hard for family and friends to accept
And let go of the one who is gone
Now one is free from sickness and pain
Our angel in the sky
One is gone in flesh
But their spirit lives on
As we sit back and think about
The good times we had with one and
All that they have done
A smile will then come
If one should start feeling themselves coming down
Stop for a moment, look up, and say
A few words to
Our angel in the sky

Blessed with smiles and tears of joy.

In God's Hands

In God's hands everything is a blessing
Yes, we all will have our ups and downs
But the outcome will be a joyful sound
In God's hands things are blessed
Turn your problems over to him
And he will carry you through
In God's hands
One may go through a test
Test of strength, faith, and Bible base
Believing in God, knowing that he's there
Looking down on us every way
In God's hands

Believe in God.

A Heavy Load

When one has a lot
Too much to carry
A heavy load
What should one do?

As time goes on
And months have passed
One's goal and strive
Is to remove them
A heavy load

I know God will not
Put too much on us
That we can't handle
So with his help, I'm asking
"Heavenly Father, Lord of thee"
I give this load to you
Father God, I put this things
In your hands
They are too heavy for me
A heavy load

Let the fear go.

Bursting Out

Bursting out the fear
That one has been holding in
Scared of failure
That one may fall
Bursting out a shell, like a bird does to an egg
One has relieved themselves
Willing and wanting to
Try new things
Bursting out a loud cry
Don't know who to turn to or
Where you should go
But if you will only
Fall to your knees, bursting
Out a loud call to your
Heavenly Father
He will hear you, grab you
And lead you in the right direction
But one must believe and hold on
Build themselves up stronger with faith
So one can burst out

Blessed to have a strong heart.

My Dream

I have a dream today
It's to be all that I can be
To bring my kids up
In the right direction
To be a leader
Not a follower
I have a dream today
That all things are possible
If you ask for it
It shall be given
We shall unite as a whole
I'm asking for help
Dear Lord of thee
help me with my dream
To have a clear mind
Positive attitude and
To be all that I can be

Be grateful.

God Calling

While out walking about
Many things cross one mind.
"What is my job?"
Our Heavenly Father wants me to be
"My calling you will see," said our
Heavenly Father Lord of thee
While trying to succeed
One may fall, we all will have
trials and tribulations
While trying to reach our call
At times, one may not believe
that this is their job
Our Heavenly Father
Is calling them to be
That job may look strange or not fit for thee
But it's not our place to judge or point fingers
This is God calling, he blesses you to be

Tell yourself, "I can."

How Can I

How can I let go?
The fear to proceed
The gift and ability to accomplish
Overcome the fear of failure
How can I?
Make my dreams come true
Stop the dreamland
Of wanting to live that dream
With God's help, all things are possible
One must have strength
Of faith and believe in him
Most of all, drop to your
Knees, speak to the Lord within
Believing in him and yourself
So you can succeed
How can I?

Miracles can and will happen.

What Should I do?

Heavenly Father, Lord of thee
A crying-out heart I give to thee
What should I do?
I'm having problems too heavy to bear
Have dos and don'ts
What should I do?
I'm confused, twisted all up inside
Don't know which way I should turn or go
What should I do?
Father God, please take heed
For I will bear
Guide me, lead me out of this mess
Send me down the road
To happiness
What should I do?

God will pick me back up.

A Crying-Out Heart

Heavenly Father, Lord of thee
A crying-out heart I give to thee
My heart is full of tears
I don't understand why me
I know that happiness
Doesn't last always, hard times
We all must face
And it's how we handle these
A crying-out heart, I cry to thee
Lord, bring me back closer and
Stronger to thee
I am asking you to show me,
Guide me, lead me the way, to
The road of a strong heart, I will obey
Father God, as I dry up my tears
Give me a positive attitude
As well as a made-up mind
For my crying-out heart
I will put it away
Believing in faith, so I'll become
Stronger and stronger each day
A crying-out heart

Get on your knees and pray.

When I Woke Up This Morning

When I woke up this morning, I forgot to pray
I got dressed so that I can start my day
While at work, my day was stressful,
frustrating and my body was tired
But when the next morning came
I paused for a moment
got on my knees and prayed
Thank you, Lord, for blessing me to see another day
Walk with me, Lord, be by my side as I start my day
Bless me to have a peaceful great day
This is what I prayed
When I woke up this morning

Tell yourself, "The Lord will guide me."

A Strong Hold

A strong hold is my love
My love that I have for you
A tight squeeze and pressing
So that no one else can break through
Yes, we have had our
ups and downs
That's something we all go through
But those pieces have been
picked up and mended
back together
A strong hold is like a
Chain that is hard to break
And that chain of love
That I have is holding
Strong on you

Grow stronger.

My Love

My love for you is undying
No one can take that away
My love for you is everlasting
That is how I want that
To stay
Now I know that you are
Far away
But to me, you're close
To my heart
And as the days and nights
Are passed away
My love for you, darling
Grows stronger each day

God opened my eyes.

When the Time Is Right

When the time is right
I shall stop looking
For someone who is faithful
And understanding
When the time is right
I shall stop looking
For someone who will
Be there when I need him
Now I know that we just met
But to me, it feels like I've
Known you for a long time
And I'm glad to say
That the time is right
And I have stopped looking
Because I've found you
And maybe one day
When the time is right
You can stop looking
And make me your wife.

We all must have strong faith.

I Want to Say I Love You

I want to say I love you
But I'm afraid you'll laugh
And if you laugh
When I tell you
It would break my heart in half
I want to do more things with you
Because I love you so,
And if I ask you
To do these things
I will die if you say no
I want you to love me
As much as I love you
And if you say you hate me
I don't know what I would do
My love for you is like a stream
That runs forever true
And that stream of love will never
Run dry as long as I have you

Happiness and joy from the Lord.

Someone Asked

Someone asked "Do you love him?"
I responded, yes, to the fullest
Someone asked "Is he there for you?"
I responded, yes, all the time
He's always walking by my side
Someone asked "Have you ever slipped away?"
I replied, yes, I have fallen back
I got back on my feet and asked for forgiveness
That person then said
"He's a good man, what's his name?"
I stated, I'm not talking about a man in flesh
I'm talking about the man up above
Our Heavenly Father
He'll walk by our side, lead you, guide you
In the right direction
When one is going through
Hardship or when situations occur
Our Heavenly Father
Will fix them f or you
He'll be right on time

I will keep trying.

Jump, I Have You

While listening to a pastor preach
He spoke upon the Lord
Jump, I have you
When one goes through hardships
And their worries begin
Jump, I have you
When your funds are low
And debts are high
Jump, I have you
One may think that he's forgotten all about them
But the Lord will be there, he'll be right on time
Not by your will but by his
One must remove the doubts, fear, and release the stress
Believe in the Lord at all times
Build up your faith as well
When feeling discouraged, wanting to back away
Stop for a moment, then say
I will jump into the hands of the Lord
He has me at all times

Within

My desire is to keep pushing forward.

My Little Prayer

God, you know my needs
Only you can help me
When I'm feeling down,
You are there to pick me up
When I'm in need and my
Burden gets tough
You step in and take the load

Sometimes I wonder
"Am I asking for too much?"
Not a moment too soon
Or too late
I know that my
Needs will be met
My little prayer to you
"Dear God, help me, guide me
And lead the way, for I will take heed
Father, show me the way"

We serve a magnificent God.

So That You Can

So that you can have a positive attitude
Trust in God
So that you can become stronger
Fall to your knees and pray
So that you can
Take the worry and stress away
Believe in God
Build up your faith, walk on the path of righteousness
Proceed to accomplish
Of reaching your goals
Knowing that our Heavenly Father is there
Everywhere that one goes
He'll lead you in the right direction
So that you can
Reach out and grab your blessings
Because he will be walking by your side
So that you can…

Love is all around me.

Stains We Once Had or Have

It's a part of life that we all have had some stains
It can get on your clothes, carpet, chairs, etc.
When stains get on one clothes
One may use bleach or stain removal
Stains can also get inside of one body
Stains from using drugs, addiction of taking it
Stains from being an alcoholic
Addiction of drinking too much of
Many things can cause one to have stains
To clean up our stains, one must put them in
The man up above's hands, our Heavenly Father
He can and will remove the addictions and bad habits
That is down on thee
Stains that the Lord has cleaned up and taken away
Will allow one to have a pure heart, a lighter load to carry
And be joyful indeed
Stains taken and remove by the Lord

He's my provider.

The Value Of

Everyone and everything has a value to it
The likes and dislikes of all things an everyone
When one wants to buy a vehicle
The value of it will be determined
By the condition of it
One looks at the color, body style, shape
And the interior inside of it
One may also look to see if there's
Any scratches or dents on it
If so, the value of that vehicle will be low
We as people can also have a value on us
That goes by others' preference
Whether we are big or small, tall or short
Long hair or short, it doesn't matter
Others will base their value on their likes
But the man up above, our Heavenly Father
Has no value price on his people
He will take and accept us just the way we are
Our value will be priceless

Rise up within.

It Is You

Living in today's world
Can be hard
Finding a true friend
Can be a hard thing too
Now I've found my friend
And that friend is you
When my funds are low
And my debts are high
Who can I turn to?
What should I do?
It was the Lord and you
That helped me to get through
When I was feeling down
Hurt all inside or just
Needed a shoulder to cry on
It was the Lord and you that helped me
To get through
Your advice, helping hand, and caring heart
Friend, you must understand all of that is what carried me through
Now I know that we have had ups and downs
Friendshipwise
But with the help from the Lord
We made it through
Words cannot express how I feel
But most of all, thank you
For being you

Give thanks.

Just a little Something

Just a little something
To say "it's a pleasure to work with you"
As we sit back and make
Each other laugh and share
Our helping hands when needed
So as you sit back and relax
Think about the
Blessing from the Lord
And all what he has done for you
Remember one thing
Once again, it's a pleasure
To work with you.

Happiness is all around me.

Grandma, You Mean Everything

Grandma, you mean everything
A blessing from God
To be blessed to you
Now that we, your grandkids
Are getting older and you are too
We sit around and think about the past
When we were kids
How we would go outside and play
On a warm beautiful day
And you would be in the kitchen cooking
Windows pulled up and the smell from the food coming out
Grandma, you mean everything
If one of us would fall or get hurt while playing
It was you who we would run and cry to
You would clean the hurt spot
Bandage it up and give us a hug and kiss then say
"All right, baby, go back and play"
Now it's time for the tables to be turned around
And let us your grandkids be there and do for you
'Cause, Grandma, you mean
Everything

Love to the fullest.

Just Because

Just because you mean
The world to me
You are my everything
A blessing from the sky
You are a lifesaver
When onc is in need, the
helping hand you gave
Just because you
Are my best friend
A special person to me
No one can take your place
Or be like you
You are love in some many ways
That will never end
Just because
You are my mother
That special person you are
Just because

I'm grateful.

"Is It Meant for Me?"

I sit back and asked myself
"What is meant for me?"
I have dreams and goals that I'm
Striving for, hoping I'll be able to reach
But what is keeping me back
The sense of fear and failure
Fear that I may not make it
And failure that I might not pass
Is it meant for me?

To join the air force
So I can "aim high"
The navy
So I can "full speed ahead"
The Army
So I can "be all that I can be"
Or maybe
The marines
I can be one of the "few proud ones"
Is it meant for me?
The desire that I have for these goals are
Strong, hoping I'll be able to succeed
Praying that I can be one of the ones to say:
"Yes, it was meant for me"

Blessings will be given to all.

A Special Blessing

A special blessing
High praise and glory
Goes out to all the mothers
I know times can be
Hard for some
Especially the ones that
Must take the
Place of the absent dads
Who weren't there or
Others who just don't care
A special blessing goes
Out to the mothers
Who sat up in the night
With their sick ones
Causing some to miss their income
Words itself cannot express
How wonderful it feels
To have moms that was there
Giving love and care
From this day on, each day if one can
Let's show some appreciation
By giving hugs and kisses
Or maybe a thank-you gift
Not because it's Mother's Day
But because moms are our special blessing

Happy Mother's Day

A new start for myself.

The Wings of an Angel

Heavenly Father, Lord of thee
Help me to grow strong
With my needs
As I lift my hands
Up to thee, let the wings of an angel
Wrap them around me
Lord, help me to grow strong in faith
Take all the negative thoughts
And feelings away
Deep down inside, I want to find me, the real me
Better yet, the way I used to be
With a cheerful heart, a happy smile
And a positive attitude
All things are possible
If one believes in it
So from this day forward, I will tell myself these words
"I know I can"
And with the strength and power
From you, Lord
Let the wings of an angel
Lead me, guide me, show me the way
Amen, Amen, Amen

Blessings will be given to all.

About the Author

The author, Shamarel, was born in Virginia, but she was raised up in Georgia. She's married and has three kids of her own along with two stepdaughters. She loves to spend as much time as possible with her family. She loves to travel, and on her chill days, she'll sit back and watch her fish in her aquarium. She works at a state institution in Georgia. She has been there for many years.